Prayer Expedition at Epworth by the Sea

Dr. Richard M. Wright

WestBow
PRESS®
A DIVISION OF THOMAS NELSON
& ZONDERVAN

Holy Bible New International Version, copyrighted 1973, 1978, and 1984 by International Bible Society

WestBow Press books may be ordered through booksellers or by contacting:

WestBow Press
A Division of Thomas Nelson & Zondervan
1663 Liberty Drive
Bloomington, IN 47403
www.westbowpress.com
1 (866) 928-1240

ISBN: 978-1-9736-2887-3 (sc)
ISBN: 978-1-9736-2889-7 (hc)
ISBN: 978-1-9736-2888-0 (e)

Library of Congress Control Number: 2018905990

Print information available on the last page.

WestBow Press rev. date: 5/31/2018

Dedication

To Epworth by the Sea's guests who come for spiritual growth and Christian education while relaxing among God's beautiful creation on this sacred ground on Georgia's coast.

May your prayer expedition and discovery be uplifting and fruitful as you draw closer to God and discern the divine plans for you! God's richest blessings to you as you make this trek!

Contents

Foreword

Whether it is your first visit or your hundredth to Epworth by the Sea, this guide to prayer will greatly enrich your experience of this unique setting. Out of his own personal journey of prayer at Epworth, Rich Wright has designed a resource that combines inspiring history, illuminating scripture, and intentional prayer.

Epworth already means so much to so many of us. It has shaped the lives of children, youth, and adults for generations. Now we have a fresh way to explore Epworth through the fourteen different stops on the prayer expedition outlined by Dr. Wright.

I thank Rich for his response to the nudging of the Holy Spirit in the direction of this guide to prayer. I have been blessed by it and encourage its use by all who wish to open themselves to spiritual refreshment and renewal at Epworth by the Sea.

Bishop R. Lawson Bryan
The South Georgia Annual Conference
The United Methodist Church

Acknowledgments

I acknowledge Jesus Christ as my Lord and Savior! I am still amazed that God called me to be an ordained elder within The United Methodist Church. The last twenty-plus years of pastoral ministry have been a great journey!

I thank God for the wonderful weather on the days that I took the pictures for this book. The grounds are always spectacular. The grounds are even more beautiful in the spring and summer, when the azaleas and other flowers are in full bloom.

This project would never have gotten off of the ground if it had not been for Rev. Dr. Craig Rickard. While doing a book-signing event at the 2015 South Georgia Annual Conference, Craig and I talked about writing. He suggested that I embark on a book for spiritual growth that included Epworth by the Sea. What a great idea! Thanks, Craig, for the genesis that resulted in this prayer book.

Of course, without the majestic setting of Epworth by the Sea, this book would not exist. I am grateful for those who founded this great retreat center. I imagine that they believed great things would happen on this campus. There have been literally thousands of children and adults who have given their lives to Christ, have had their Christian faith nurtured, and continue to guide others toward a deeper relationship with God through Christ. I thank the many people who keep this center going by reaching out to many people and groups who visit this wonderful place each year.

I thank the Epworth by the Sea staff for their assistance in making this project a reality. I especially want to thank Joel Willis, the president and chief executive officer, and Rev. Wayne Racz, the director for spiritual formation, church relations, and development. The encouragement and assistance you provided were tremendous and contributed mightily to this project.

I want to thank each person who uses this book to guide their prayer journey around the campus of Epworth by the Sea. I pray that you will learn about the various prayer stops and that you will enjoy a deeper relationship with God through Christ as you use each stop as the means through which you can receive God's grace on your spiritual journey.

Introduction

Why This Book?

I am filled with excitement every time I come to St. Simons Island and that beautiful place called Epworth by the Sea. The excitement is because I know that I will be able to draw closer to God. This connection has been made possible because of the various events and programs that I have attended over the years. As the former superintendent, Rev. Dr. Charles Adams, commented each time he talked about Epworth by the Sea, "Epworth by the Sea is a great place to be!"

I attended some of these programs for continuing education as a pastor, spending many hours in classrooms or one of the auditoriums for training. Other programs provided me some time to enjoy the campus and the surrounding communities of St. Simons and Brunswick.

Driving onto the campus, you realize that you are approaching a special place as you pass under moss-covered live oaks. Rolling the windows down, you realize that the hustle and bustle of the world is drowned out by the wind blowing gently through those trees and the birds singing. Then you see it—the main gate welcoming you to the sacred ground called Epworth by the Sea!

On each visit, my excitement grows as I see friends from over the years who are there, and as I participate in the event for which I am there. Over the last few times that I visited Epworth, I also explored the various monuments and plaques located all over the campus. I noticed that there were several places where I could stop for a time to contemplate whatever was on my mind. On each visit, I used different places to pray and meditate. I sensed God's presence each time. But, more important than this sense of divine presence, I sensed God speaking directly to me and the situations that I found myself in.

I felt that I was being moved toward writing this book, but I had other tasks on my plate. Being a United Methodist pastor, I discounted the urge to write because I really did not have time to write another book.

Well, I was wrong. When Rev. Dr. Craig Rickard said that I ought to write this book, my reaction was, "How did he know about this thought I had about an Epworth prayer book?" When Rev. Wayne Racz walked over to our book-signing table at one of our annual conferences, Craig mentioned this project to him. He said, "That would be a great idea!" That moment was when this book was born in earnest!

I have to admit that this project became much larger than I had initially envisioned. It has taken longer than I thought it would too. I have enjoyed each moment of working on this book and visiting Epworth again to take the pictures of the stops.

Each of these prayer stops has some history behind it that most visitors to Epworth don't know about. I pray that you will take a minute to learn about each spot's historical significance. However, I know that these locations across the Epworth campus are best used for prayer and meditation.

A Brief History

Epworth by the Sea is located on the Gascoigne Bluff of the Frederica River. It is a ministry owned and operated by the South Georgia Annual Conference of The United Methodist Church. The property was purchased on October 29, 1949, and the gates opened to serve the world in 1950.

I have found Epworth by the Sea to be one of the finest Christian retreat centers in the Southeast. Its mission is to provide a Christian place for fellowship, worship, and study. It is able to do this with a large campus of over one hundred acres that houses dining rooms, motel-style rooms, cabins, auditoriums, meeting rooms, a gymnasium, a preschool, playgrounds, athletic fields, and conference offices. These accommodate the many ministries, events, programs, and study groups that use the retreat complex throughout the year.

The Gascoigne Bluff extends from the F. J. Torras Causeway Bridge to the bend in the Frederica River at the D. Abbott Turner Lodge, on the northern end of the Epworth campus. The bluff is named for Captain James Gascoigne. Gascoigne commanded the *Hawk*, which was the sloop-of-war that provided escort security for the first British settlers establishing Fort Frederica in 1735. This strategic bluff offered naval vessels a first landing place upon entering the harbor. Because of its geography and importance for naval security, the bluff was given the title of "The Gateway to St. Simons Island."

This ground is also important to world and American Methodism because Reverends John and Charles Wesley were at Fort Frederica. John was responsible for the colony's religious affairs. Charles served as the minister to the occupants of the Fort Frederica settlement. Although it cannot be proven, I like to think that the Wesleys may have actually walked on this ground.

Charles returned to England in July 1736, while John returned in December 1737. In 1739, John and Charles Wesley began to do field preaching in England, which meant they were not preaching in churches or cathedrals but out in the fields and streets. It is from this kind of preaching and establishing other methods for spiritual growth that the Methodist movement sprang forth.

The land along the Gascoigne Bluff swapped owners several times after 1735. It housed large plantations, farming operations, lumber mills, and even a US Navy headquarters. In 1880, Norman W. Dodge built St. James Union Chapel, which was later renamed Lovely Lane Chapel. The lumber mills were closed around 1903. In 1927, the property was purchased as a winter home by Mr. and Mrs. Eugene W. Lewis of Detroit. They operated a large farm and established several gardens on the grounds. However, in the early 1940s, their farm was closed because the farm workers went to work in Brunswick for higher wages.

In 1949, the South Georgia Annual Conference of the Methodist Episcopal Church purchased a large part of the property to establish a Christian retreat center. On July 25, 1950, Bishop Arthur J. Moore officiated over the consecration and opening of the new Methodist center. It was named Epworth by the Sea in honor of the boyhood home of John and Charles Wesley in Epworth, England.

Epworth by the Sea has grown since its start in 1949. However, it still stands as a memorial to Methodism and provides those who visit with a link from our present time to the past history of the Methodist movement throughout the world and within the United States.

Prayer and Meditation

Prayer is not some complex task that we engage in. Prayer, in its simplest form, is sharing with God what is on your heart and mind, then listening to what God needs you to take from this moment of conversation.

At each of the locations I describe in this prayer expedition, you will find places to sit, like benches, or you can use the ground to stretch out and look up at the sky. The position you use to pray is up to you! I have used both of these prayer positions, depending on how I felt at the time. I often found that I spent much more time in prayer than I thought or planned for. I also found that each time was filled with meaningful dialogue with God. I would arise from that spot as a renewed Christian, filled with divine power and encouragement to go and do what I sensed God was asking me to do.

In these prayer times, I discovered that I was more than a conqueror. I am a child of God, and no one can steal that joy from me!

Meditation is a little more intense than prayer. It involves spending several minutes to focus on a specific situation for which you need guidance from God. It also involves using breathing to create this focus. Meditation helps to calm our minds about an intense topic or to give us a positive perspective on an uncomfortable situation. Be prepared for this to take some time! When I meditate, I am reminded that I didn't get into this situation quickly, and sometimes it takes more than one conversation with God to hear a certain course of action to take toward resolution.

With each stop on this prayer path, I will share some history. I will also provide some scripture in which to center your mind and spirit. I end each stop with a prayer. I invite you to use the scripture and prayer at each stop. But if you have a scripture passage that comes to mind or you want to pray on your own, please feel free to do so. I also encourage you to carry a Bible with you, or have a Bible app on your smartphone. I discovered that sometimes the Holy Spirit whispers some great guidance to me through scripture or remembering a story from the Bible.

Whatever reason you have for using this prayer guide, I pray that you find time to converse with God about your life and your situation while you visit Epworth. I also pray that you receive whatever it is that God has for you. I hope that you, like me, leave Epworth with answers that will help you in your relationships, occupation, and church.

Ready to Start?

I call this an expedition because you are going to discover some things about Epworth that you didn't know. I pray that you will also discover more about God and yourself while you spend quality and quantity time in prayer and meditation.

The places along this expedition call out to you to come and enjoy your time with God. Most of the stop locations are accessible by walkways or paved roads. Therefore, you will have an easy walk across the campus to get to each of the prayer stops.

The walk is not just to get to each of the prayer stops. I encourage you to relish the walk by slowing down and taking in all of the natural beauty that God has provided us on this picturesque piece of ground. Allow yourself to truly experience all that God is putting before you, from the trees to the river to the history to the animals to the people that you will encounter. All of them are present to support you in your prayer time.

Enjoy the spiritual path during your prayer expedition, because God has provided the path and God will walk with you for the entire journey! May God's richest blessings be poured out upon you as you embark on this spiritual endeavor! Let's get started on this fantastic expedition!

Prayer Expedition Map

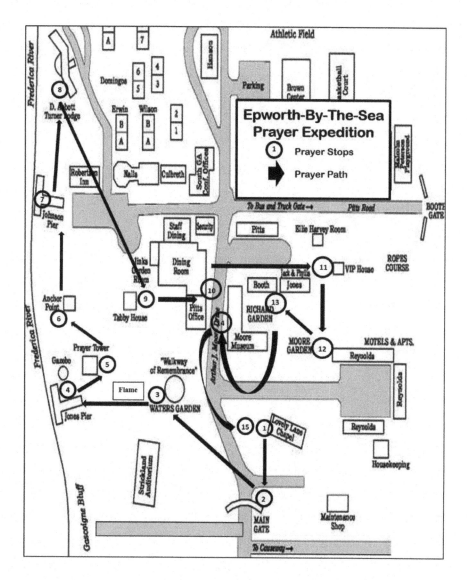

Prayer Expedition Locations

Stop 1
Lovely Lane Chapel

We begin our prayer expedition at Lovely Lane Chapel. Many years ago, I learned that before you embark on any great or important undertaking, you ought to invoke a blessing from God. So we begin our expedition at Epworth's chapel.

History

Lovely Lane Chapel is the oldest standing church building on St. Simons Island. It is located just inside the main gate. It is surrounded by pines and palms. If the chapel is open, then you have to take a look inside. You can spend some time in prayer inside or outside of Lovely Lane Chapel.

This beautiful chapel was constructed in 1880 by Norman W. Dodge. It was originally named St. James Union Church. Between 1911 and 1949, the chapel was used as a recreation center for the island's residents. In 1949, the chapel was reconsecrated when the vast property was purchased to construct a retreat center for Georgia Methodists.

The chapel was then renamed. It gets its name from a chapel in Baltimore, Maryland, where, in 1784, American Methodism was founded at the Christmas Conference. It was at this first general conference that Thomas Coke ordained Francis Asbury and appointed him as co-superintendent with himself. During this conference, the new American Methodist denomination adopted the name the Methodist Episcopal Church.

With this name, Lovely Lane Chapel reminds us of the meager beginnings of Methodism in the United States, and that it is up to each Methodist Christian to continue striving for God's ways in our world. Based on the work of these few itinerant Methodist preachers, Methodism spread across the United States. American Methodism's growth can be attributed to the people who followed God's guidance to share the good news of Christ with others. This continues today through local United Methodist churches, where we gather to worship, fellowship, and conduct ministries.

Lovely Lane Chapel is a beautiful edifice that stands out because of its whitewashed exterior. The chapel's interior is simple, with wooden walls, pews, and pulpit. The modest exterior and interior serve as a reminder of the simple beginning of American Methodism.

This chapel has some wonderful stained glass windows. They are made of old English art glass. The works of art glass help us to remember that everything that God makes is good.

Lovely Lane Chapel is open to the public for Sunday worship services. The times for these services can be found in each of Epworth's hotel rooms or by asking the front desk. It can also be reserved for wedding ceremonies. What is remarkable is that Lovely Lane can seat up to 150 people for its worship services, which is hard to believe when you see the interior.

Scriptural Focus

As we begin our prayer journey here at Lovely Lane Chapel, I am reminded that Christianity is a social religion whereby we worship, fellowship, and learn with each other. Therefore, this passage from Hebrews 10:25 came to mind: "Let us not give up meeting together, as some are in the habit of doing, but let us encourage one another—and all the more as you see the Day approaching."

With this location and scripture guiding us, the focus at this stop is on the local church, our worship of the Holy Trinity, and our fellowship with each other. Prayer and meditation can be seen as mini worship services during which we adore God and give God thanks for all of it.

Prayer

Gracious God, I thank you that you have called me into your church. It is a tremendous blessing to know that you called me into the local church that I attend. You have given me a place in which to serve you, my faith community, and the world with the spiritual gifts that only you could have bestowed upon me. We pray that you will strengthen the body of Christ to share the good news of Christ with all people. I pray that in the local churches, you will be glorified by the various ministries that touch the lives of many people. Empower me to continue the fellowship with other saints, which makes me stronger. Lovely God, guide me to use my spiritual gifts, church ministries, and Christian fellowship to transform my little piece of the world. In the powerful name of the Christ I pray. Amen.

Next: Stop 2, Main Gate

Stop 2
Main Gate

The main gate stands as the greeter to all who come onto the Epworth campus. The moss-covered live oaks and the archway tell us that we are coming onto sacred ground. It is on this sacred ground that lives are changed spiritually, emotionally, and physically. This was emphasized by Bishop Arthur J. Moore when he said, "Epworth by the Sea has been built with the hope that through Christian atmosphere, friendly fellowship, and spiritual dedication, this may be a place where many shall purpose to make Jesus Christ supreme."

History

Just inside the gateway arch, we see the monument about John Wesley, the founder of Methodism. It reminds us of the historical importance of this place on the Gascoigne Bluff on the Frederica River. Just a short distance from Epworth stand the ruins of Fort Frederica, where General James Oglethorpe and the Wesleys, both John and Charles, came to offer protection to the new colony and to offer pastoral care to these new colonists.

Although we have no definitive proof that John or Charles Wesley walked on these grounds, we know that John's time in Georgia was significant in his spiritual growth as an Anglican priest and as a Christian. After his time in Georgia, John Wesley returned to England to continue drawing closer to God. Part of building this relationship with God was writing and preaching on salvation and the Methodist way. From this growth, Wesley became the founder of Methodism. He eventually saw the need for ordained Methodist preachers in the new colonies. John Wesley ordained Thomas Coke to go to America to share the good news and ordain Francis Asbury as a co-superintendent of the American Methodist preachers.

With this thought about Wesley, Coke, Asbury, and Methodism, we can see how this retreat center stands as a place where people can spiritually grow. This growth is seen in some people accepting Christ as Lord and Savior, others recommitting themselves to their Christian faith, and still others maturing in their faith through the various programs and events offered throughout the year. As the archway informs people, this is a retreat center that offers Christian fellowship, worship, and study as ways to embrace God's means of grace and to become more like Jesus Christ.

Scriptural Focus

As you stand here looking at the main gate, it serves as an invitation to continue your spiritual journey. With this guide, I invite you to continue this growth through prayer and meditation at each expedition stop.

This gate encourages me to remember that Jesus Christ is the one who sacrificed himself, instead of me, on the cross of Calvary. With his life, death, resurrection, and ascension, Jesus built the body of Christ, which is the Christian church. Jesus is still expanding the Christian church with you and me. I see this gate as God's tool to teach me about the church.

As I approach scripture and the teachings of Jesus, I am guided to Matthew 21:13, where Jesus says, "My house will be called a house of prayer." The intent of Epworth is just that. However, we are called to take this same intent to our local churches.

The prayer focus for this stop is on the great cloud of witnesses in our pasts who helped to guide us toward an encounter with Christ in a house of prayer. We also remember how the Wesleys transformed the world through their failures and successes within Methodism.

Prayer

Sustainer of all people, I stand amazed at how you have orchestrated humanity's history. You have taught me many lessons about life. You have surrounded me with a cloud of witnesses to your great love for humankind. Help me to learn from the failures and successes of the past. As I remember them, help me to know that you were present with all people who came to the saving grace of Christ and are now part of your family. I ask you to continue to lead people to this sacred ground and to houses of prayer around the world to become a part of the body of Christ and to continue their spiritual growth. Guide them to be the Christians you need each to be as your kingdom continues to grow here on the earth. Use this retreat center and our local churches to put forth your ideas and ways in which we are to glorify you in our prayers, presence, gifts, service, and witness. In the loving name of Jesus we pray. Amen.

Next: Stop 3, Waters Garden

Stop 3
Waters Garden

This stop brings us to an area where there are several monuments: the Waters Garden fountain, the World Methodist Evangelism Institute's globe sculpture with flame, and the Walkway of Remembrance. There are also paver bricks and park benches near the Strickland Auditorium to commemorate the service of many different people. This large area is a great place to have a seat and look at the fountain or out over the marshes of Glynn.

History

The predominant structure is the Waters Garden. The fountain is surrounded by a brick paver walkway that is called the Walkway of Remembrance. The brick pavers serve as reminders of the people who helped to make us who we are. It is especially a beautiful spot to come and remember deceased family and friends.

The fountain is the center of our attention, and it serves as a spiritual focal point too. With the sound of the water coming up and out of the fountain and then cascading down into the pool, visitors are welcomed with a feeling of renewal and cleansing.

You can take time to walk around the fountain and read each of the brick pavers. You may find one with a person's name you know. If you do, I pray that this time will bring you comfort and peace, especially as you reminisce about your relationship with that person. Even if you do not know any of the people memorialized on these brick pavers, I hope that you will sense what these people mean to someone in the world.

This garden is visited quite often when people have events in the Strickland Auditorium. Even if you did not intend to stop at the fountain, it seems that you are drawn to it: a place where you can think of people whom you encountered during your lifetime, especially people who have made some kind of impact on your life. May you enjoy the peaceful atmosphere of this garden.

Scriptural Focus

Water has a significant place in the Bible and in the life of Jesus. In Jesus's life, water was where God recognized his Son in public, during John the Baptist's baptism of Jesus. Luke 3:22 states that a voice from heaven said, "You are my Son, whom I love; with you I am well pleased."

Jesus also performed his first recorded miracle in the New Testament by turning water into wine at a marriage feast in Cana. In John 2:11 we find, "This, the first of his miraculous signs, Jesus performed at Cana in Galilee. He thus revealed his glory, and his disciples put their faith in him."

As I look at the water, I am reminded more impressively about my baptism. At each baptism that I witness, I am invited to remember my baptism. At this prayer location, I can remember my baptism by thinking about what baptism means to me and how I am to live up to my baptism vows by doing what God is inviting me to do for the kingdom.

Other scripture passages may come to your mind at this location, but there are two that come to my mind. The first is found in Acts 2:38. Apostle Peter preaching his first sermon on the day of Pentecost: "Repent and be baptized, every one of you, in the name of Jesus Christ for the forgiveness of your sins. And you will receive the gift of the Holy Spirit."

The second one is the Great Commission in Matthew 28:19–20, which comes from Jesus himself: "Therefore go and make disciples of all nations, baptizing them in the name of the Father and of the Son and of the Holy Spirit, and teaching them to obey everything I have commanded you. And surely I am with you always, to the very end of the age."

These scripture passages motivate me to focus on how I am moving through the salvation process. As this focus continues, I am chided to remember my baptism and my place within the body of Christ. The Walkway of Remembrance encourages me to remember the people who touched my life and helped to lead me to a deeper relationship with God through Christ.

Prayer

Wonderful Creator, thank you for sending Christ to save the world. I especially thank you that he saved my soul. I thank you for the Holy Spirit that directs my steps, even on this day. I pray that I will heed your directions as I do my best to live the kind of life that you desire me to live. I pray that you will forgive me when I stumble along the path that you have placed before me. Empower me to be the baptized servant that the kingdom on earth needs. I thank you for placing saints in my life who demonstrated your kind of love to me. I pray that I am just as good an example to others as those saints were to me. Help all of your people to work out their salvation in the way that will build up your kingdom. On earth as it is in heaven. In the name of my Savior, Jesus Christ, I pray. Amen.

Next: Stop 4, Jones Pier and Gazebo

Stop 4
Jones Pier and Gazebo

We finally make it to the Frederica River and Gascoigne Bluff by coming to the Jones Pier and its gazebo. There are three piers on the Epworth campus that extend over the Frederica River. The Jones Pier is unique among the three because it is the only pier named after an influential businessman.

History

In the late 1940s, Bishop Arthur J. Moore and the South Georgia Annual Conference retreat center commission members stood on this bluff and looked out over the salt marshes of Glynn County. They may have remembered the poem by Georgia poet Sidney Lanier about these marshes, but they did have in mind the establishment of a retreat center for Georgia Methodists to use in the future.

In order to make this dream into reality, Bishop Moore needed the assistance of many Methodist supporters. One of these supporters was Alfred W. Jones Sr., who handled property affairs for the Sea Island Company. He would eventually become the president and chairman for the Sea Island Company and a major developer of the Georgia coastline. Mr. Jones helped Bishop Moore and the Georgia Methodists purchase a large part of the closed Lewis plantation in 1949.

This pier and lovely gazebo are located on the southern part of the Epworth campus to commemorate Mr. Jones's efforts to develop the Georgia coastline and to help place the retreat center at this location on St. Simons Island.

The views from this location are magnificent. You can see the salt marshes in their full splendor during low tide. During high tide, you can see the river rise enough for boat travel. Occasionally, you can see dolphins swimming in the harbor and along the Gascoigne Bluff. At sunrise or sunset, the view is even more impressive! However, anytime is a good time to stop in this locale and offer a prayer to God

Whether at high tide or low tide, may your time at this location be very pleasant. You can take a seat in the gazebo on those very hot Georgia summer days to pray. Or you can do what Otis Redding sang about, "sitting on the dock of the bay," by sitting on the pier itself. I find that the sunsets are very nice to take in from either place. More importantly, the prayers that you offer up to God are heard by God and answered through Christ and the Holy Spirit!

Scriptural Focus

There are many biblical passages that speak about rivers. From the time of creation, when a river watered the garden of Eden, to the river of the water of life in the New Jerusalem, rivers of water are important. It is the same here for our prayer journey. The passage that continues to dominate my prayer time at this location comes from the latter allusion, the New Jerusalem. This passage is found in Revelation 22:1–5:

> Then the angel showed me the river of the water of life, as clear as crystal, flowing from the throne of God and of the Lamb down the middle of the great street of the city. On each side of the river stood the tree of life, bearing twelve crops of fruit, yielding its fruit every month. And the leaves of the tree are for the healing of the nations. No longer will there be any curse. The throne of God and of the Lamb will be in the city, and his servants will serve him. They will see his face, and his name will be on their foreheads. There will be no more night. They will not need the light of a lamp or the light of the sun, for the Lord God will give them light. And they will reign for ever and ever.

With this passage and the stunning sight from this location, the focus of our prayer is on the river and what the River of Life means for us. As a Christian, I know that our hope is in the New Jerusalem. No matter what your situation may be, this hope can compel you to strive for this promise in all that you do for yourself, your family, and your little part of the world, including your church. I hope that you cling to this hope during the good and not-so-good times of your life.

Prayer

Almighty God, it is a joy that I am able to be here in this place. You have created this river and this retreat center to allow people to enjoy a respite from the world's chaos and personal struggles. You have also created this time for me to reflect on my relationship with you. As memories flood over my mind, I stand in awe of how much your love has meant to me. You have enabled me to touch the lives of many people, from family to friends to acquaintances. As I have touched their lives, they have touched me in many ways. I look forward to the day when all I will do is praise you in paradise. Until that happens, I pray for your enduring presence wherever I find myself, doing whatever it is that I am engaged in. As you guide me with your Holy Spirit, I pray that my life, words, and actions are pleasing to you and helps your kingdom to prosper. In the name of my Lord, Jesus. Amen.

Next: Stop 5, Prayer Tower

Stop 5
Prayer Tower

The prayer tower dominates the area that overlooks the bluff at the Frederica River on the western edge of the Epworth campus. You can hear the carillon as it plays hymnal music at the top and bottom of each hour during the day. The large cross on top of this edifice reminds us that this is a place for us to remember who our Savior and Lord is. He is Jesus the Christ!

History

This prayer tower was the endeavor of South Georgia United Methodist Men. The biggest promoter of this the project was George A. Wright, whose name is honored on the prayer tower. (No, I am not in any way related to George A. Wright.) The tower was completed in 1982, after Mr. Wright passed away. But his leadership within the United Methodist Men of South Georgia helps to make this tower a reality.

The tower calls out to all people when it rings out. The striking music touches your soul with hymns that are rich with theology. More importantly, it provides a tool by which your soul becomes more open to God during your prayer time in and around this location.

This stop means that you are one-third complete with the prayer expedition. How is it going thus far? Also with this stop at the prayer tower, we are reminded how important it is for us to stop several times daily to offer a prayer to God.

You can sit among the many live oaks that surround this tower, or you can sit closer to the river on one of the many benches along the river walkway. I find that the best way to use this location is to focus on the large cross as a beacon of hope in our lives.

Scriptural Focus

Apostle Paul wrote in 1 Thessalonians 5:16 that we are to "be always joyful," which can be achieved when we continually pray to God and give God thanks for whatever situation we find ourselves in.

Sometimes it is hard to always be joyful because we allow our situations to overwhelm us, particularly when we perceive the situation as a negative one. Paul reminds us that we can always pray to God about anything that is on our hearts and minds.

I am encouraged by reading the Psalms. In the 150 psalms, I find myself quite often. Sometimes I am on the mountaintop, praising God for a victory in my life. Other times I am in the deepest valley, wondering where God is. You have been there too, right?

But don't fall into despair. In Psalm 40:1 we read, "I waited patiently for the Lord; he turned to me and heard my cry." Thank God for hearing our prayers! However, the psalmist teaches us that many times we have to be patient with our prayers and our expectations of how God answers those prayers. I have learned that the answers from God are yes, no, or wait.

"Yes" is great to get when it comes immediately after we have prayed. This is an answer we get many times from God, especially when the petition is for our best interest.

We are not particularly fond of "no" or "wait." However, we don't know the bigger scheme for our lives. God does! I have experienced and seen that there are other things that have to occur before we can encounter an answer to our prayers. Sometimes the petition is not in our best interest in the long term; therefore the answer is no.

The "wait" answer is tough because we don't know how long we have to wait. We learn from the psalmist that we are just to keep looking for the answer. I hope that as you pray at this location, you are going to hear God's answers to your prayers as you offer them up to the One who can hear and answer them!

Although I have already shared a couple of biblical passages with you, there is one more for this location. I think I would be remiss in writing this book if I didn't share this passage at some point along our journey together. The passage describes Jesus teaching the disciples to pray what we call the Lord's Prayer. Of course, I think that this title is a misnomer. I think that the prayer ought to be called "The Disciple's Prayer," since we, as disciples of Jesus Christ, are encouraged to pray this by our Lord! Matthew 6:9–13 reads:

> This, then, is how you should pray:
> 'Our Father in heaven,
> hallowed be your name,
> your kingdom come,
> your will be done
> on earth as it is in heaven.
> Give us today our daily bread.
> Forgive us our debts,
> as we also have forgiven our debtors.
> And lead us not into temptation,
> but deliver us from the evil one.'

Our focus at this location is on our prayers. The prayer tower serves as a call to prayer. May we not only pray "The Disciple's Prayer," but also pray for ourselves and those whom we are concerned about. For some of those people, we know their names. Others are just faces in the crowds of the world. All are in need of divine intervention in their situations, just like us!

Prayer

Heavenly Father, thank you for giving me a place to rest and pray. I ask you to forgive me for not living a life that is continually joyful. You know that I have encountered many struggles in my life, and I have been hurt. In the midst of my physical, emotional, and spiritual pain, I could not find the joy that you wished for me to enjoy. I thank you for not giving up on me! As I reflect on my life, I can see how your hand was constantly with me. What a joy! As I come to the end of this prayer, I realize that life will not always be joyful, but I can always rejoice for you are with me!

Dr. Richard M. Wright

Thank you so much for showing me such beautiful love. Lifting up my heart to you through Christ. Amen.

Next: Stop 6, Anchor Point

Stop 6
Anchor Point

S top 6 is, in my view, the oddest monument on our prayer expedition. It is odd because it is not on any of the normal walkways provided across the Epworth campus. This monument has palms and two benches to sit on, but it sits way back from the riverfront on a hillcrest near the prayer tower.

History

I like this stop because of where it sits and the direction it is facing. On the hillcrest, you can see to the left and right as well as forward. This is a great place to sit and pray while the sun is going down. I can see why the Pierce family saw this place as the anchor point!

You are near the prayer tower and can easily hear the chiming of hymns at the top and bottom of the hour. You can see others walking across the campus, and you might see a friend you haven't seen in a while. You can even work on your suntan because the location is somewhat bare.

The most important point about this location is that its name and perspective toward the west aids you in thinking about in whom you put your trust. If you are like me, you put your trust in Jesus Christ, who sacrificed himself on the cross instead of us having to pay the price for our sins.

Jesus is the anchor who provides salvation for our souls and forgiveness for our sins. As we approach the divine anchor, we can know that Jesus receives our prayers from the Holy Spirit and then intercedes on our behalves with God the Father in heaven! Is there a better anchor than that?

Scriptural Focus

I cannot help but think of Hebrews 6:19 as I sit at this place. The Pierce family used it on the plaque found here too. "We have this hope as an anchor for the soul, firm and secure."

Not only does an anchor hold a boat when the seas are calm, but it really works hard when storms come. Therefore, the focus at this point is that the anchor holds in the storms of life. As the writer of Hebrews teaches us, it is secure and firm. The only anchor that can do that is Jesus.

The focus is to allow this divine anchor to hold you firm and secure in the Christian faith. Christ is the answer to many questions in our lives. As the anchor, Christ helps us when we don't know what questions to ask. I hope that you are firmly anchored by the love and sacrifice of Christ.

Prayer

Gracious and loving God, in you I find not only grace, but a God that I can approach with my life's issues. I thank you so much for listening to me, but I really thank you for giving me an anchor in this life, named Jesus Christ. Sometimes I forget that you are there for me in the good and the tough times. Forgive me, I pray, for trying to handle my life on my own. Guide me to trust you even more than I do right now. Laying all of my problems at your throne of grace in the name of Christ. Amen.

Next: Stop 7, Johnson Pier

Stop 7
Johnson Pier

Just like the Jones Pier earlier, the Johnson Pier extends over the Frederica River, but near the northern edge of the Epworth campus. This pier is a great place to fish from when the tide is high! It is also a good place to pray.

This pier extends further than the Jones Pier. This means that you can experience other things on this pier. The wind is a little stronger, but it is usually not too strong to enjoy the salty breeze. You can also see farther up the northern riverbank, and you have a better view if the dolphins are swimming in the river.

History

This pier is named after Rev. Thomas Halliburton Johnson Sr. Rev. Johnson began his ministerial career in 1952 at Martha Bowman Methodist Church in Macon, Georgia. In 1956, he was appointed to the two-point charge of Bloomingdale and Meldrim. His next appointment came in 1959, when he was moved to White Bluff Methodist Church in Savannah. His other Methodist appointments included Baxley First (1964), Park Avenue in Valdosta (1968), Statesboro First (1972), and Perry First (1976). He served the South Georgia Annual Conference as the Thomasville district superintendent in 1981 and as the Waycross district superintendent in 1988. He retired from active ministry in 1993.

Rev. Johnson was honored with the naming of this pier because of his service to Epworth as its superintendent from 1985 to 1988. His many years of ordained ministerial service continue to be celebrated when each person comes out onto this pier for sport fishing, sightseeing, and praying. I thank Rev. Johnson for his past service and for his service to the South Georgia Annual Conference since retirement, because he has not slowed down since retiring.

Scriptural Focus

As I sit on this pier, I am reminded of what God did in the beginning. This was captured in Genesis 1:1: "In the beginning God created the heavens and the earth." As you watch the river, regardless of the tide, you can see the beauty of the water as it ebbs and flows. The waves interact with the riverbank by embracing the soil and the plants that are along the bank.

When I think of the tides of the ocean, which influence the depth of the river at this point, I am brought back to God creating the heavens and the earth. God thought about the position of the planets, and especially the size and location of the moon relative to the earth. The relationship of the earth and the moon causes the tides to ebb and flow. As the waters rise and fall in this harbor river, the different animals interact within its waters. From fish to dolphins to waterfowl to other animals, God created each and God found them to be good. I pray that you will enjoy this beauty, whatever you are able to experience.

Our focus for this prayer stop is on God's creation. God created all and found it to be good in the beginning. It is up to people to maintain the planet so that our future generations will have the same opportunities to enjoy nature and its benefits, and especially to experience the blessings of the creation that God made.

Prayer

Creating God, I come before you to thank you for creating the universe and all that is in it. Thank you for food, clean water, shelter, fresh air, clothing, animals, and the various plants. I also ask you to forgive me for not taking care of the world's resources as well as I should have. Come and transform my heart and mind so that I may be a better steward of these resources you have provided. Thanks for hearing my prayer for your creation and for helping me to appreciate all that you have given to the world. Lifting this prayer up to you in the name of Christ. Amen.

Next: Stop 8, Turner Lodge

Stop 8
Turner Lodge

We have reached the halfway point of our prayer journey. I congratulate you on making it this far. I pray that you are being blessed in your prayer time.

This stop brings us to the veranda of the D. Abbott Turner Lodge. This building is the northernmost building on the Epworth campus. It is also the largest and youngest hotel on Epworth. The veranda is found on the back of the lodge. It faces the west for a view out over the river and the Glynn marshes.

History

D. Abbott Turner lived in Columbus, Georgia, and was a central business figure in the Georgia business community. He was a leader of several corporations and was also very active in philanthropy. This reputation and business experience made him a great asset in building a Christian retreat center in southeast Georgia.

Bishop Arthur J. Moore enlisted Mr. Turner to help in this endeavor. Mr. Turner was with Bishop Moore from the beginning in 1945, when the conversation came up about a retreat center. He was a major factor in purchasing the property and developing the vision for Epworth. He was also a major financial contributor to turn this vision into reality.

The prayer location at the Turner Lodge is on its veranda. By following the walkway from the Johnson Pier, you will find your way to the veranda.

The nice thing about this stop is that the veranda is enclosed and has rocking chairs to sit in. I always like using the rocking chairs because they make me slow down to pray and also to rest and relax.

But beware! I fell asleep one afternoon in one of those rocking chairs and had a very restful nap! Unfortunately, I missed a part of the event that

I was there to attend. God must have known that I needed that time with him and rest for my body and mind. Thank you, God!

The lodge, as of the writing of this guide, is the most recent major building project at Epworth. It provides hotel rooms for the many events held at Epworth. We are appreciative that the building plans included the veranda where we have stopped to pray!

Scriptural Focus

We work so hard to make a living, to make a family, and to become the best Christians we can be. All of this means … hard work. We work hard, but rarely do we take time to slow down, rest, and relax. I am reminded of this when reading Psalm 127:2:

> In vain you rise early
> and stay up late,
> toiling for food to eat —
> for he grants sleep to those he loves.

Sitting here on the veranda, I think about what God told us to do. In Exodus 34:21, God taught us that we work for six days and ought to rest on the seventh day, regardless of the time of year. So, sitting on the veranda in a rocking chair at the largest hotel on the Epworth campus, let us think about rest, sleep, and relaxation.

Regardless of your reason for being at Epworth, I pray that you find rest and relaxation during your visit. This prayer expedition trek will not last long. I pray that you will have a good night's sleep when it is time for you to slumber!

Prayer

God of all, I thank you for this place called Epworth. I also thank you that I can stop in the hustle of the day to pray to you. You have watched over me in the past. I am confident that you will be present with me in the present and the future. I ask you to watch over me for the rest of the day. I thank you for this day and for the night that is to come soon. I pray that you will empower me with a good night's sleep so that I can face the tasks of tomorrow. I also thank you for giving me this opportunity to walk on this prayer expedition. Give me strength to complete this prayer walk, but also to have trust in you to answer all of these prayers. In the name of my Lord and Savior, Jesus Christ, I do pray. Amen.

Next: Stop 9, Tabby House

Stop 9
Tabby House

This prayer stop takes us back to the 1800s! This stop is where one of the oldest buildings on St. Simons is located. The Tabby House gives us a glance at life on the island in the late nineteenth century.

History

This house was originally built around 1806 as a cabin for slave labor on the Hamilton plantation, and was constructed with slave labor. There are still some original parts of the house that exist today.

The house is called the Tabby House because of the material that makes up the house's walls. Making tabby is quite labor intensive, but it was a great substitute for brick in the nineteenth century because clay was not readily available on the island. The process starts with crushing and burning oyster shells into quicklime. The quicklime is combined with more oyster shells, sand, and water. The mixture is poured and tamped into wooden forms called *cradles*. The cradles remain in place until the material hardens, which can take several days depending on the thickness of the material. The cradles are used to build up walls in layers until they reach the required height.

Tabby was used for floors, foundations, columns, roofs, and chimney bricks in nineteenth-century construction. If the tabby was used for floors, it was normally replaced after about ten years because of wear and chipping.

When the plantation was bought in 1949, there were four slave cabins still on the property. The Tabby House is the last remaining slave cabin. It has undergone intensive renovations since the Methodists purchased the Epworth campus. In 1995, the Tabby House was near complete collapse. It was decided to work toward restoring the cabin as closely as possible to its original design. As you can see from the photo, the cabin has been fully restored and is in use today.

The cabin is used for banquets, wedding rehearsal dinners, luncheons, small receptions, and meetings. It is also used to educate people about life on the island in the 1800s. School groups and youth groups learn about tabby, plantation life, and the island's history.

The cabin, for me, helps to link our present to the past. It reminds me of the failures and successes of our forefathers and foremothers, which we are able to build upon. It is important for us to learn about the past so that we do not make the same mistakes again.

As I think about this, I am taken back to the familiar saying that is attributed to the Spanish philosopher, essayist, poet, and novelist George Santayana. "Those who cannot remember the past are condemned to repeat it." I pray that we don't make those same mistakes, but that we are able to build up God's kingdom.

Scriptural Focus

These educational endeavors and Santayana's remark further remind me about our relationship with God. The psalmists expressed it aptly in their hymns.

Psalm 119:4–8 teaches:

> You have laid down precepts
> that are to be fully obeyed.
> Oh, that my ways were steadfast
> in obeying your decrees!
> Then I would not be put to shame
> when I consider all your commands.
> I will praise you with an upright heart
> as I learn your righteous laws.
> I will obey your decrees;
> do not utterly forsake me.

In Psalm 143:10, we find:

> Teach me to do your will,
> for you are my God;

may your good Spirit
lead me on level ground.

Both passages encourage us to learn God's ways and to do them. As you pray at this place, think about how you learn more about God and your relationship to him through Christ.

But don't stop there! Ask yourself, "Am I doing what I am learning?" If you are, congratulations for pursuing God's calling in your life. If not, then what do you hear from God about how to make the desired changes in your life? Prayer is one-third talking to God and two-thirds listening to God!

Prayer

All-knowing God, thank you for education and for those who teach me. You have given the gift of teaching to some wonderful people. I praise you for their service to you and to the world. As I have learned your precepts for living, I pray that I honor you with my life and service to others. As I look at this restored Tabby House, I am reminded of the countless number of people who occupy the great cloud of witnesses that surround each believer. I am overwhelmed at how you have used each one to share the love of Christ with others, especially with me. Thank you for using me as one of those saints who glorify you through my service to others. Help me not only to learn your ways, but to work toward doing your will in my life. Surround me with people who will encourage me to continue moving forward toward being the Christian servant that you desire me to be. Praying for continued learning and service in the body of Christ. Amen.

Next: Stop 10, Front Porch

Stop 10
Front Porch

Once again we come to a place that has rocking chairs for our use! We find ourselves at the front porch of the Pitts Office and the dining rooms.

Inside the building, there are Epworth offices, a gift shop, and dining rooms. Outside on the front porch, we can take another prayer break while relaxing in red rocking chairs. You might see someone you know pass by! Or you might make a new friend as you discuss life and the latest news and the event that you are here to attend!

History

While sitting at this location, we can see more moss-covered live oaks surrounding the office building. What I see the most when I am sitting here are people walking by.

The office is named after Miss Margaret Pitts. Her parents, Mr. and Mrs. W. I. H. Pitts, were devoted Methodists. Through investments in Coca-Cola, the Pitts family were able to financially support Epworth and Methodist educational institutes in Georgia via the Pitts Foundation. After her parents' deaths, Miss Margaret directed the foundation. In the 1970s, the foundation enabled several buildings to be constructed on the Epworth campus. The Epworth trustees honored Miss Margaret by naming the office after her.

Most people stay on the Epworth campus for conferences, ministry groups, or some other kind of event. At any given time, some are out walking, sightseeing, running, or biking in the area. The people come from many parts of the world. They are drawn to Epworth because of its beauty and influence on world Methodism. These are God's people whom God loves.

Scriptural Focus

As I think about these people, I cannot help but go to the most famous New Testament passage, John 3:16: "For God so loved the world that he gave his one and only Son, that whoever believes in him shall not perish but have eternal life."

As we take a rest break here at our tenth prayer stop, let us think about how God loves us in spite of ourselves. This love is so great that God wants to forgive the mistakes that we call sins. It is through this forgiveness that we are able to receive a new life filled with hope that comes directly from God. That new life is what is called by Apostle John "eternal life!" I pray that you have experienced this divine moment.

Our prayer at this stop returns us to thinking about our relationship with God. If God loves us, then we ought to love ourselves and our neighbors. This is so hard most of the time. God can empower us to extend this love to ourselves and others because of the divine power that God grants us through the divine-human relationship. I pray that you are able to use this power to overcome any hindrances to your love for God, yourself, and others.

Prayer

Loving Father in heaven, I thank you so much for forgiving my mistakes against you, myself, and others. Through Christ, you have given me wonderful gifts of salvation, family, friends, and your church. As I continue to pray during this prayer expedition, I ask you to continue being with me by letting your Holy Spirit correct my thoughts, characteristics, words, and actions. Help me to share the good news of Christ with others so they can encounter Christ and enjoy the hope that he provides. Help me to give forgiveness to those who have hurt me. This is so hard to do, but you can guide me to use the right words and attitudes to not only do this, but to actually mean it. Thank you for hearing my heart as I pray this prayer. I look forward to seeing how you are going to answer this prayer, along with the other prayers that I have prayed during this expedition journey. I am praying this prayer through the wonderful name of my Lord and Savior, Jesus the Christ. Amen.

Next: Stop 11, VIP House

Stop 11
VIP House

This stop brings us to the VIP House. It is called this because it is used for special occasions or for lodging of dignitaries. It is often used by brides on the night before their weddings at Lovely Lane Chapel.

There is a plaque near the front door that honors an influential figure in American Methodism, Bishop Arthur J. Moore.

History

The house was built in 1880 as the office for a sawmill that was located on the property. Today, it is another Epworth building that connects the past with our present.

To pray, you can sit on the front porch in a rocking chair or use a bench located in the front yard. Either way, you have a beautiful view of the live oaks and the Moore Garden.

Bishop Moore's biography is too long to include in this book. I recommend that you learn more about his lasting legacy within American and world Methodism. However, I will share some high points during his service as a bishop in the Methodist Church.

Rev. Dr. Arthur James Moore was elected bishop at the 1930 General Conference of the Methodist Episcopal Church, South (MECS) in Dallas, Texas. He was assigned to the Pacific Coast. He also was the episcopal leader who provided oversight of Methodist missionary activities in several countries in Asia, Europe, and Africa.

He was a member of the Committee on Interdenominational Relations and Church Union of the MECS from 1934 to 1939. In 1934, Moore helped to create *The Upper Room*, which is a worldwide daily devotional guide dedicated to spiritual growth.

After the uniting conference in 1939 that merged three branches of Methodism into the Methodist Church, he was assigned to the Atlanta episcopal area, which covered the state of Georgia. While serving as the bishop of Georgia, he was also president of the Board of Missions and Church Extension of the Methodist Church. He became the organizer and first president of the Board of Evangelism for the Methodist Church.

His influence continued to grow as he served as interim president of the all-women's Wesleyan College in Macon, Georgia, in 1941, and as a board member of several colleges, universities, and hospitals. He wrote several books and provided servant leadership on many Methodist general agencies and boards. For readers of this book, perhaps his greatest impact is felt in the establishment of Epworth by the Sea in 1949.

In 1960, Bishop Moore retired. However, he did not retire from ministry. He continued to provide leadership, guidance, and support to many ministries around the world until he died on June 30, 1974.

We thank Bishop Moore for his extraordinary leadership to Methodism. However, our prayer focus at this point is on marriage between a man and a woman, in which the husband-wife relationship can flourish. It begins with a wedding, but that ceremony is only a few minutes in duration. The prayer of the wedding is that the marriage will last for a lifetime. Bishop Moore was supported by a loving wife, whom we will learn about in our next stop.

Scriptural Focus

Apostle Paul gave some instructions for a good marriage in 1 Corinthian 7:3–6:

> The husband should fulfill his marital duty to his wife, and likewise the wife to her husband. The wife's body does not belong to her alone but also to her husband. In the same way, the husband's body does not belong to him alone but also to his wife. Do not deprive each other except by mutual consent and for a time, so that you may devote yourselves to prayer. Then come together again so that Satan will not tempt you because of your lack of self-control.

It is in this way that the marriage can last. Tough times will come, but that is when time in prayer will help the husband-wife relationship endure. It also shows that there is work that has to be performed for the marriage to overcome the struggles that will come along at some time.

Prayer

All-knowing God, thank you for creating relationships when you first created humanity. Help me to have a deeper relationship with you first. I ask that you will draw me closer to my spouse through prayer and intimacy. As I hope that my love for you grows each day, help me to love my spouse (or significant other) more each day too. Remove any temptations that may exist for both of us. When tough times come, encourage us to come together with you to decide how to overcome those challenges. I pray that these tough times do not force us apart from each other. Grant your Holy Spirit to guide us in walking on the path that you have set for each of us. Empower us to support each other in the holy endeavors that you are calling each of us to participate in. I pray that you are glorified in our marriage (or relationship). I lift this prayer up to you in the name of Jesus the Christ. Amen.

Next: Stop 12, Mattie Moore Garden

Stop 12
Mattie Moore Garden

J ust a short walk from the VIP House is the garden that bears the name of Bishop Arthur J. Moore's wife. Arthur married Martha McDonald, who was known as Mattie, on April 26, 1906. They had 5 children.

History

In 1909, Arthur confessed Jesus as his Lord and Savior. He immediately began to preach the good news of Christ.

Mattie, his wife, was present through all that her husband experienced as an evangelist, pastor, and episcopal leader. She was a wife who was behind the scenes while her husband was in the spotlight. She died in 1964.

In the midst of this garden is a marble monument that tells us about Mattie. It says:

> She was an unusually gifted lady with a settled faith and a quiet heart who lived a radiant life. Her unfaltering trust, her wise judgments and her consecrated service made her a source of inspiration and strength to all who knew her.

> We thank thee for the majesty of the heavens. We rejoice in the sky born music of the night of stars; the hush of the dawn when the world wakens to the warmth of the sun which causes the earth to bud and blossom; for the bounty of creation; the loveliness of nature and the beauty of a garden for all this we lift our hearts in thanksgiving.

The garden that bears her name is a beautiful spot. There are a few benches that you can sit on to pray. No matter which one you choose or if you choose to stand, you will be surrounded by the awesome sight of many horticultural delights found in the trees, bushes, grass, and flowers.

God had to provide the right amount of rain for these plants to offer up the wonder of blooms. The blooms bring butterflies, bees, and birds that enjoy the awaiting nectar and fruit.

I am sure that Mattie would have loved this garden named in her honor. I am sure that you will enjoy praying here in this place.

Scriptural Focus

Each time I sit in this garden, I think about rain. It may spoil our outdoor plans, but it is essential for growth. The rain helps the plants, but it does much more. It cleanses the air we breathe. It provides us water to drink. The sound of falling rain is a great way to fall asleep on a sleepless night.

I am taken to two passages about rain. Deuteronomy 11:13–15 tells us, "So if you faithfully obey the commands I am giving you today—to love the Lord your God and to serve him with all your heart and with all your soul—then I will send rain on your land in its season, both autumn and spring rains, so that you may gather in your grain, new wine and oil. I will provide grass in the fields for your cattle, and you will eat and be satisfied."

Wow, what a great promise! This divine promise being fulfilled is dependent upon our response to the divine hope. We must love and serve God in order for the rain to fall when it needs to. Thank God that we can respond in trust in the Triune God, who is faithful to keep the many divine promises that we find in the Bible.

The second passage comes from Jeremiah 14:22: "Do any of the worthless idols of the nations bring rain? Do the skies themselves send down showers? No, it is you, O Lord our God. Therefore our hope is in you, for you are the one who does all this."

Our hope is in God to send the rain and to give us a place in his church. We can cling to this hope through our faith in Jesus Christ, who secured our place in his church, and through our trust in the Holy Spirit, who bestows the appropriate spiritual gifts that we need to use in our various local church ministries.

Prayer

Compassionate God, thank you for your creation. Thanks for all of the plants, animals, and people. I especially thank you for the rain that does so much for our planet. As you send rain for the world, I ask you to rain down your Holy Spirit upon me to discern my place within your church. Equip and empower me with this divine rain to serve you so that you are blessed through my words, deeds, and ministries. Send the rain, God, for the world. I need it to cleanse my soul now. Your world needs the rain to help it to survive and grow. In Christ's name I pray. Amen.

Next: Stop 13, Richard Garden

Stop 13
Richard Garden

This prayer stop is one of the secluded locations that few know exist. The Richard Garden is behind the Moore Museum and adjacent to the Booth and Jones buildings. The hedges on the eastern side of the garden provide quietness that is great for praying.

History

History tells us that a swimming pool and a smaller garden were once located here. A decision was made to fill in the swimming pool many years ago. After that decision, Rev. and Mrs. R. J. Gisler of Lakeland, Florida, wanted to honor her parents with a lasting legacy. It was determined that a garden would be the best way.

This garden was named in honor of Mr. and Mrs. Walter Lee Richard of Atlanta, Georgia. It is a fitting memorial and location because of the Richards' close relationship with Bishop and Mrs. Arthur J. Moore. The Richards were also generous financial supporters of Epworth during their lives. On December 6, 1986, this fantastic garden was dedicated with a beautiful ceremony.

This garden, combined with the Moore Garden, provides a step into the past when there were several gardens on the Lewis plantation. The benches provide a place to take a load off of your feet. We have only two more stops on our prayer expedition.

Scriptural Focus

At the Mattie Moore Garden, our focus was on rain. Here at the Richard Garden, the focus is on the sun. Sun is needed for real growth to occur in the plants that surround this garden. Trees, grass, hedges, and flowers all need the sunlight to express their total beauty.

We need the sun as well. Sunlight helps us to have a brighter disposition and outlook on life than an overcast or dark day. The Son is also needed to provide the divine light in our lives so that we can stay on the path that God desires us to be on.

The psalmist in Psalm 84:11 reminds us:

> For the Lord God is a sun and shield;
> the Lord bestows favor and honor;
> no good thing does he withhold
> from those whose walk is blameless.

This Son, who is Jesus Christ, is always present with us, regardless of the kind of day we may be experiencing. The Son is also there in the dead of night for us to pray through to God.

Prayer

God of the sun and rain, I thank you for sending what I need each day. I praise you for being the sun and light on the path you need me to traverse life on. Be my guide as I find myself in the valleys, the mountaintops, and every point in between. Poke me when I forget that you are there to help me in making decisions that are pleasing to you. When I stumble, send your Son to show me how I can get back on the path. Allow this bright light to cheer me up on the dark days of life. Also, help me to learn and follow the ways of your Son. Thank you for your favor and honor. In Christ's name. Amen.

Next: Stop 14, Arthur J. Moore Museum

Stop 14
Arthur J. Moore Museum

This next-to-last prayer stop brings us to the largest conference-owned United Methodist museum in the world! This museum is another endeavor of Bishop Arthur J. Moore.

History

The museum was originally established in 1965 as a place to preserve the history of Georgia, St. Simons Island, and world Methodism. Since 1974, the museum has been the historical archives for the South Georgia Annual Conference of the United Methodist Church.

The museum helps us to walk back into centuries of history. Its various displays guide us through the pre-Revolutionary War era up to the present. It does this by showing us historical artifacts and providing some details about American Methodism that are often overlooked. The greatest treasure, in my opinion, is the library that is available for genealogical and scholarly research.

This museum stands as a testimony to the sharing of the Christian faith. The displays show how Christians have done this since the 1700s. From the Wesleys to Bishop Moore to us, God calls us to introduce Christ to people by the many communications techniques available. Without Christians doing this, the good news of God's love will not be able to have its intended effect—salvation offered to everyone.

Scriptural Focus

We come to praise God for the grace, hope, and love that is extended to us. We are able to respond to these great things from God because we realize the benefits that are possible in our lives because of God, Christ, and the Holy Spirit.

In Psalm 5:11 we are taught, "But let all who take refuge in you be glad; let them ever sing for joy." We are able to sing with joy regardless of our situations. The rejoicing is made possible because of the hope that comes by being in a deep relationship with God through Christ. We grow in the grace and knowledge of Christ as we endeavor to be more like Jesus each day. Even on those days when we feel that we are far from being more like Christ, we can have joy because we are God's people saved by divine grace for a wonderful purpose.

As I think about this rejoicing, I am drawn to Psalm 33:22. The hymn writer asks, "May your unfailing love rest upon us, O Lord, even as we put our hope in you."

As we rejoice in God and share the good news of Christ, we are able to receive divine love. The more divine love we receive, the more we are able to hope and trust in God, who calls us to do something great in the world whereby God is further glorified.

Prayer

Great God, I rejoice because you love me and give me a fulfilled hope. As this museum stands as a testimony to evangelism and faith-sharing, please empower me to be an evangelist in telling others about my trust in you. I pray that you are blessed as I serve you by being a blessing to others. Thank you for the saints who came before me. I want to build upon their lasting legacies. Help me to find the divine purpose that you want me to have. Empower me to strive toward not only achieving this holy purpose, but being more like Christ each day. Clothe me with your full armor so that I can sense your protection as I do your will. Thank you for listening to my prayer for I raise it up to you in the name of Jesus. Amen.

Next: Stop 15, Lovely Lane Chapel

Stop 15
Lovely Lane Chapel

Congratulations! You are right back where you began at Lovely Lane Chapel!

Why are we finishing here? Because you need to thank God for being with you during this prayer expedition. It is God's presence that helped you to proceed from one stop to another. As you encountered that holy presence, you were able to offer up prayers to Almighty God.

You may have used the prayers in this book or prayed on your own or offered a combination of the two. It does not matter which way you used. What is important is that you spent time in prayer to a God who loves you. You took time to draw closer to God!

As you prayed, I hope that you poured out your heart and that you took time to listen to God speaking directly to you. That voice could be found in your mind, in the wind, in the gurgling of the river, or in encountering nature in other ways.

I also hope that you learned about how special Epworth by the Sea really is to you and to those who visit here. I pray that you will return to Epworth soon, to visit and to pray.

Scriptural Focus

As we complete our time together on this prayer journey, I am compelled to use passages about finishing the race, like Acts 20:24 and 2 Timothy 4:7–8.

Acts 20:24 says, "However, I consider my life worth nothing to me, if only I may finish the race and complete the task the Lord Jesus has given me—the task of testifying to the gospel of God's grace."

Christians are to run the race. We are not sure where the path will take us, like this prayer expedition. But we know that God will be with us no matter where it leads us. We are to start the race by accepting Jesus as our Lord and Savior. The race is not over; it is only beginning. We are to keep running the race until we complete the tasks that God needs us to do. These tasks only end when we outrun our loved ones to the Father's home!

Apostle Paul teaches in 2 Timothy 4:7–8 what is waiting for us at the end of the race: "I have fought the good fight, I have finished the race, I have kept the faith. Now there is in store for me the crown of righteousness, which the Lord, the righteous Judge, will award to me on that day—and not only to me, but also to all who have longed for his appearing."

Congratulations on completing this spiritual task of a prayer expedition. But we have one last prayer to offer up to God before we can say that we have completed this task.

Prayer

O God, thank you for teaching me so much during this prayer expedition. I have opened myself up to you and shared things that are on my heart and mind. You have been so merciful in listening to me. You have dispensed your love to me in all of these prayers. Thank you for the revelations you have entrusted to me. Grant me your power and perseverance to accomplish all that you are asking me to do. Thank you for Epworth by the Sea and all that it means to people worldwide. I appreciate my time here at Epworth and your holy presence. Hear my prayer, O Lord, for I pray it in the name of Christ. Amen.

Epilogue

Some of you are probably wondering if I, as the author, actually made the trek of this prayer expedition. The answer is a resounding *yes*!

What Rev. Dr. Craig Rickard and Rev. Wayne Racz did not know at the time of their encouragement is that I needed to write this book. The research on the history of the various places had a calming effect on me because I enjoy reading and experiencing history.

I found that walking the Epworth campus several times to lay out the prayer expedition was physically and emotionally rewarding. I slowed down to fully experience all that Epworth's grounds could give to me. I saw things that I had not seen over many years of coming to Epworth. I felt that God was causing me to slow down to fully experience life.

There is more to experience at Epworth, from the athletic fields to the preschool to the ropes courses, that I did not include in this prayer expedition. I invite you to see all that Epworth has to offer for spiritual development!

After charting the prayer expedition path, I went to each prayer stop and actually prayed. It's hard to believe that a United Methodist pastor prayed without being in a pulpit or at a public gathering. My prayers, which I wrote down after praying, are the ones found in this book. I pray that they mean as much to you as they did to me. I also hope that they will help you on your spiritual journey toward God's throne of grace!

I found myself spiritually renewed with each prayer. I hope that you sensed the same thing that I did. I admit that I have not put all of the items from my prayers in this book, because of the deep personal nature of my petitions. I hope that you were also able to get to a deep personal level in your prayers to Almighty God.

I had stress and high levels of anxiety that I had bottled up after fifteen years of being an Airborne Ranger infantryman in peacetime and combat operations, combined with over twenty years of ordained pastoral ministry. That stress began to be reduced through this prayer expedition. I saw situations in my life and in my ministry in a different light—a more positive one! As I gained a different perspective, I was able to see how God was not only present in those situations, including the not-so-good ones, but he was continuing to move me toward many more years of parish ministry within the United Methodist Church.

As I came back to Lovely Lane Chapel at the end of the prayer walk, I spent time thinking about my relationships. The most important was my relationship with God through Christ. I know that I fall short of being the Christian and pastor that God intends for me to be. I have a long way to go on my salvation journey to perfection. But I have made progress daily to this end. This prayer expedition served as an affirmation that I am doing what God called me to do for the kingdom, and God will empower me to overcome the challenges that I will face today and in the future.

God will do the same for you. No matter what you are encountering in your life right now, God is with you. God has been preparing you for such a time as this.

Second, I thought about my relationships with those who are close to me—my family and friends. I strive to be the best I can be. My prayer time showed that I falter as well as succeed quite often. I sensed that life was a series of roller-coaster rides with highs and lows. My family and friends accept me and love me for who I am. They pray for me to continue on this spiritual expedition so that I will find out what I am to be doing for the kingdom at each pastoral appointment. I thank God for them. It is only by my relationship with God that I am able to love and enjoy time with my family and friends.

As I conclude this book, I thank God for you! You have taken time to do this prayer expedition. I prayed for you and your spiritual growth even before you started. Thank you for supporting Epworth during your visit. I hope that you will come back to Epworth soon and do this prayer walk again.

My ardent prayer is that you discovered more about God and yourself. Like Kool and the Gang sang, "Celebrate!" Tell others what you did and what it meant to you. I invite you to share Jesus Christ with others so that they can enjoy the love, peace, and joy that you have by being one of God's children.

Remember to take time to pray when you are not at Epworth. You will be greatly blessed by God. You will also be blessing God with the work you have engaged in to draw closer to God. This can only enhance your personal relationship with God through Christ.

When I conclude a worship service, I usually issue a benediction. It has become my signature benediction throughout my pastoral ministry. This is how I want to end our time together:

May the love, grace, and mercy of God the Father,
the salvation that comes only through Jesus Christ the Son,
and the most awesome power of the Holy Spirit
go with you now and forevermore.
Amen!

Select Resource List

Davis, Taylor P., "Tabby: The Enduring Building Material of Coastal Georgia" (MHP dissertation, University of Georgia, 2011). https://getd.libs.uga.edu/pdfs/davis_taylor_p_201112_mhp.pdf.

Heitzenrater, Richard P. *Wesley and the People Called Methodists*. Nashville: Abingdon Press, 1995.

Martin, S. Walter. *Epworth: A Mission by the Sea*. St. Simons Island, Georgia: The Board of Trustees Epworth by the Sea, 1987.

New Georgia Encyclopedia. "Arthur J. Moore." http://www.georgiaencyclopedia.org/articles/arts-culture/arthur-j-moore-1888-1974.

New Georgia Encyclopedia. "D. Abbott Turner." https://www.georgiaencyclopedia.org/file/12964.

New Georgia Encyclopedia. "Epworth by the Sea." https://www.georgiaencyclopedia.org/articles/arts-culture/epworth-sea.

Norwood, Frederick A. *The Story of American Methodism*. Nashville: Abingdon Press, 1974.

Norwood, Frederick A. *Sourcebook of American Methodism*. Nashville: Abingdon, 1982.

Selecman, Charles Claude. *The Methodist Primer*. Nashville: Tidings, 1955.

South Georgia Annual Conference. "Bishop Arthur J. Moore." https://
www.sgaumc.org /bishoparthurjmoore.

Stevens, Abel. *A Compendious History of American Methodism.* New York:
Eaton & Mains, 1854.

About the Author

Dr. Richard M. Wright is a Christian, accomplished author, and dynamic speaker. He currently is a pastor in the South Georgia Annual Conference of the United Methodist Church, serving as the senior pastor of Central United Methodist Church in Fitzgerald, Georgia.

His educational endeavors include a master of divinity degree from Candler School of Theology at Emory University in Atlanta, Georgia, and a doctor of ministry degree in evangelism and missions from Austin Presbyterian Theological Seminary in Austin, Texas.

Prior to becoming a pastor, Dr. Wright served as an Airborne Ranger infantryman in the US Army's rapid deployment units. He is a combat veteran who earned the Bronze Star and the Combat Infantryman Badge during Operation Desert Storm in Iraq.

His first book, *Stop the Church's Revolving Doors*, was successful in helping churches to increase their membership and worship attendance by building personal relationships. His second book, *Help, I'm Lost*, aided relationship building by helping individuals learn more about the salvation process, whereby they could enter into a personal relationship with God through Jesus Christ.

His passion for sharing the good news of salvation through the divine-human relationship guides him in leading churches. This drive continues with this book, in which he gives practical insight and application of prayer, the spiritual discipline designed to draw us closer to God.

You can check out Dr. Wright's website at www.drrichardmwright.com and follow him on Twitter @DrRichardWright.

Printed in the United States
By Bookmasters